SPIRITUAL LETTERS

By

FENELON

SPIRITUAL

LETTERS

By Francis Fenelon

**Fredonia Books
Amsterdam, The Netherlands**

Spiritual Letters

by
Francis Fenelon

ISBN: 1-4101-0895-3

Copyright © 2006 by Fredonia Books

Reprinted from the original edition

Fredonia Books
Amsterdam, The Netherlands
http://www.fredoniabooks.com

All rights reserved, including the right to reproduce
this book, or portions thereof, in any form.

CONTENTS.

Letter
1.—The Advantage of Humiliation.................................... 3
2.—How to bear Suffering, so as to preserve our peace......... 3
3.—The Beauty of the Cross 5
4.—The Death of Self.. 6
5.—Peace lies in Simplicity and Obedience......................... 8
6.—The True Source of Peace is in the Surrender of the Will 10
7.—True Good is only reached by Abandonment................. 10
8.—Knowledge puffeth up. Charity edifieth 11
9.—We are not to choose the manner in which our blessings shall be bestowed 12
10.—The Discovery and Death of Self................................... 14
11.—The Sight of our Imperfections should not take away our Peace.. 17
12.—Living by the Cross and by Faith 18
13.—Despair at our Imperfections is a greater Obstacle than the Imperfection itself... 19
14.—Pure Faith sees God alone 20
15.—Our Knowledge stands in the way of our becoming wise... 21
16.—Those who endeavor to injure us are to be Loved and Welcomed as the Hand of God...................................... 22
17.—Quietness in God our True Resource 24
18.—True Friendships are Founded only in God 25
19.—The Cross a Source of our Pleasure............................... 26
20.—The Absence of Feeling and the Revelation of Self no sufficient Cause of Distress... 27
21.—The Imperfection of others to be borne in Love............. 29
22.—The Fear of Death not taken away by our own Courage, but by the Grace of God.. 30
23.—Sensitiveness under Reproof the Surest Sign we Needed it 32
24.—Imperfection only is Intolerant of Imperfection............ 33
25.—We should Listen to God and not to Self-love................ 35
26.—Absolute Trust the Shortest Road to God...................... 36
27.—The Time of Temptation and Distress is no time to form resolves 37
28.—Who has Love, has All.. 38
29.—Weakness preferable to Strength, and Practice better than Knowledge... 39
30.—Beware of the Pride of Reasoning; The True Guide to Knowledge is Love... 42
31.—The Gifts of God not to be Rejected on Account of the Channel that brings them 45
32.—Poverty and Spoliation the Way of Christ..................... 46
33.—The Will of God our only Treasure............................... 48
34.—Abandonment not an Heroic Sacrifice, but a Simple Sinking into the Will of God.. 49
35.—Daily Dying takes the Place of Final Death.................. 50
36.—Suffering belongs to the Living, not the Dead............... 51
37.—The Limits of our Grace are those of our Temptation 51
38.—Resisting God an Effectual Bar to Grace....................... 52
39.—God speaks more effectually *in* the Soul than *to* it.......... 54
40.—The Circumcision of the Heart...................................... 55

SPIRITUAL LETTERS

By

FENELON

SPIRITUAL LETTERS.

LETTER I.

The advantages of humiliation.

I PRAY often to God that He would keep you in the hollow of his hand. The most essential point is lowliness. It is profitable for all things, for it produces a teachable spirit which makes everything easy. You would be more guilty than many others if you made any resistance to God on this point. On the one hand, you have received abundant light and grace on the necessity of becoming like a little child; and on the other, no one has had an experience fitter to humiliate the heart and destroy self-confidence. The great profit to be derived from an experience of our weakness, is to render us lowly and obedient. May the Lord keep you!

LETTER II.

How to bear suffering so as to preserve our peace

As to our friend, I pray God to bestow upon him a simplicity that shall give him peace. When we are faithful in instantly dropping all superfluous and restless reflections, which arise from a self-love as different as possible from *charity*, we shall be set in a large place even in the midst of the strait and narrow path. We shall be in the pure liberty and innocent peace of the children of God, without being found wanting either towards God or man.

I apply to myself the same counsel that I give to others, and am well persuaded that I must seek my own peace in the same direction. My heart is now suffering; but it is the life of self that causes us pain; that which is dead does not suffer. If we were dead, and our life were hid with Christ in God, (*Col.* iii. 3,) we should no longer perceive those pains in spirit that now afflict us. We should not only bear bodily sufferings with equanimity, but spiritual affliction also, that is to say, trouble sent upon the soul without its own immediate act. But the disturbances of a restless activity, in which the soul adds to the cross imposed by the hand of God, the burden of an agitated resistance, and an unwillingness to suffer, are only experienced in consequence of the remaining life of self.

A cross which comes purely from God, and is cordially welcomed without any self-reflective acts, is at once painful and peaceful; but one unwillingly received and repelled by the life of nature, is doubly severe; the resistance within is harder to bear than the cross itself. If we recognize the hand of God, and make no opposition in the will, we have comfort in our affliction. Happy indeed are they who can bear their sufferings in the enjoyment of this simple peace and perfect acquiescence in the will of God! Nothing so shortens and soothes our pains as this spirit of non-resistance.

But we are generally desirous of bargaining with God; we would like at least to impose the limits and see the end of our sufferings. That same obstinate and hidden hold of life, which renders the cross necessary, causes us to reject it in part, and by a secret resistance, which impairs its virtue. We have thus to go over the same ground again and again; we suffer greatly, but to very little purpose. The Lord deliver us from falling into that state of soul in which crosses are of no benefit to us! God loves a cheerful giver, according to St. Paul (2 *Cor.* ix. 7); ah! what must be his love to those who, in a cheerful and absolute abandonment, resign themselves to the entire extent of his crucifying will!

LETTER III.

The beauty of the cross

I CANNOT but wonder at the virtue that lies in suffering; we are worth nothing without the cross. I tremble and am in an agony while it lasts, and all my convictions of its salutary effects vanish under the torture, but when it is over, I look back at it with admiration, and am ashamed that I bore it so ill. This experience of my folly is a deep lesson of wisdom to me.

Whatever may be the state of your sick friend, and whatever the issue of her disease, she is blessed in being so quiet under the hand of God. If she die, she dies to the Lord; if she live, she lives to Him. *Either the cross or death*, says St. Theresa.

Nothing is beyond the necessity of the cross but the established kingdom of God; when we bear it in love, it is his kingdom begun, with which we must remain satisfied while it is his pleasure. You have need of the cross as well as I. The faithful Giver of every good gift distributes them to each of us with his own hand, blessed be his name! Ah! how good it is to be chastened for our profit!

LETTER IV.

The death of self

I CANNOT express to you, my dear sister, how deeply I sympathize with your afflictions; but my grief is not unmixed with consolation. God loves you, since He does not spare you, but lays upon you the cross of Jesus Christ. Whatever light, whatever feeling we may possess, is all a delusion, if it lead us not to the real and constant practice of dying to self. We cannot die without suffering, neither can we be said to be dead, while there is still any part in us which is alive. That death with which God blesses the soul, pierces even to the dividing asunder of soul and spirit, and of the joints and marrow. He who sees in us what we cannot see, knows full well where the blow should fall; He takes away that which we are most reluctant to give up. Pain is only felt where there is life, and where there is life, is just the place where death is needed. Our Father wastes no time by cutting into parts which are already dead; if He sought to continue life, He would do so, but He seeks to destroy, and this He can only accomplish by cutting into that which is quick and living. You need not expect Him to attack those gross and wicked desires which you renounced forever, when you gave yourself away to Him, but He will prove you, perhaps, by destroying your liberty of soul, and by depriving you of your most spiritual consolations.

Would you resist? Ah! no! Suffer all things! This death must be voluntary, and can only be accomplished to that extent to which you are willing it should be. To resist death, and repel its advances, is not being willing to die. Give up voluntarily, then, to the good pleasure of God, all your reliances, even the most spiritual, whenever He may seem disposed to take them from you. What fearest thou, O thou of little faith? Dost thou fear that He may not be able to supply to thee from Himself, that succor which He takes away on the part of man? And why does He take it away, except to supply it from Himself, and to purify thee by the painful lesson? I see that every way is shut up, and that God means to accomplish his work in you, by cutting off every human resource. He is a jealous God; He is not willing you should owe what He is about to perform in you, to any other than to Himself alone.

Give yourself up to his plans—be led whither He will by his providences. Beware how you seek aid from man, when God forbids it—they can only give you what He gives them for you. Why should you be troubled that you can no longer drink from the aqueduct when you are led to the perennial spring itself from which its waters are derived?

LETTER V.

Peace lies in simplicity and obedience

CULTIVATE peace; be deaf to your too prolific imagination; its great activity not only injures the health of your body, but introduces aridity into your soul. You consume yourself to no purpose; peace and interior sweetness are destroyed by your restlessness. Think you God can speak in those soft and tender accents that melt the soul, in the midst of such a tumult as you excite by your incessant hurry of thought? Be quiet, and He will soon be heard. Indulge but a single scruple; to be scrupulously obedient.

You ask for consolation; but you do not perceive that you have been led to the brink of the fountain, and refuse to drink. Peace and consolation are only to be found in simple obedience. Be faithful in obeying without reference to your scruples, and you will soon find that the rivers of living water will flow according to the promise. You will receive according to the measure of your faith; much, if you believe much; nothing, if you believe nothing and continue to give ear to your empty imaginations.

You dishonor true love by the supposition that it is anxious about such trifles as continually occupy your attention; it goes straight to God in pure simplicity. Satan is transformed into an angel of light; he assumes the beautiful form of a scrupulous love and a tender conscience; but you should know by experience the trouble and danger into which he will lead you by vehement scruples. Everything depends upon your faithfulness in repelling his first advances.

If you become ingenuous and simple in your desires, I think you will have been more pleasing to God than if you had suffered a hundred martyrdoms. Turn all your anxieties toward your delay in offering a sacrifice so right in the sight of God. Can true love hesitate when it is required to please its well-beloved?

LETTER VI.

The true source of peace is in the surrender of the will.

REMAIN in peace; the fervor of devotion does not depend upon yourself; all that lies in your power is the direction of your will. Give that up to God without reservation. The important question is not how much you enjoy religion, but whether you will whatever God wills. Humbly confess your faults; be detached from the world, and abandoned to God; love Him more than yourself, and his glory more than your life; the least you can do is to desire and ask for such a love. God will then love you and put his peace in your heart.

LETTER VII.

True good is only reached by abandonment.

EVIL is changed into good when it is received in patience through the love of God; while good is changed into evil when we become attached to it through the love of self. True good lies only in detachment, and abandonment to God. You are now in the trial; put yourself confidently and without reserve into his hand. What would I not sacrifice to see you once more restored in body, but heartily sick of the love of the world. Attachment to ourselves is a thousand times more infectious than a contagious poison, for it contains the venom of self. I pray for you with all my heart.

LETTER VIII.

Knowledge puffeth up; charity edifieth.

I AM happy to hear of your frame of mind, and to find you communicating in simplicity everything that takes place within you. Never hesitate to write me whatever you think God requires.

It is not at all surprising that you have a sort of jealous ambition to advance in the spiritual life, and to be intimate with persons of distinction who are pious. Such things are by nature very flattering to our self-love, and it eagerly seeks them. But we should not strive to gratify such an ambition by making great progress in the religious life, and by cultivating the acquaintance of persons high in honor; our aim should be to die to the flattering delights of self-love, by becoming humble and in love with obscurity and contempt, and to have a single eye to God.

We may hear about perfection without end, and become perfectly familiar with its language, and yet be as far from its attainment as ever. Our great aim should be, to be deaf to self, to hearken to God in silence, to renounce every vanity, and to devote ourselves to solid virtue. Let us speak but little and do much, without a thought as to whether we are observed or not.

God will teach you more than the most experienced Christians, and better than all the books that the world has ever seen. And what is your object in such an eager chase after knowledge? Are you not aware that all we need is to be poor in spirit, and to know nothing but Christ and Him crucified? *Knowledge puffeth up;* it is only *charity that can edify.* (1 Cor. viii. 1.) Be content with charity, then, alone. What! is it possible that the love of God, and the abandonment of self for his sake, is only to be reached through the acquisition of so much knowledge? You have already more than you use, and need further illuminations much less than the practice of what you already know. O how deceived we are, when we suppose we are advancing, because our vain curiosity is gratified by the enlightenment of our intellect! Be humble, and expect not the gifts of God from man.

LETTER IX.

We are not to choose the manner in which our blessings shall be bestowed.

You know what God requires of you; will you refuse? You perceive that your resistance to the drawings of his grace, arises solely from self-love: will you suffer the refinements of pride, and the most ingenious inventions of self, to reject the mercies of God? You who have so many scruples in relation to a passing thought, which is involuntary and therefore innocent, who confess so many things that should rather be dismissed at once, have you no scruples about your long-continued resistance to the Holy Spirit, because He has not seen fit to confer the benefits you desire, by a channel which was flattering to your self-love?

What matter if you received the gifts of grace as beggars receive bread? The gifts themselves would be neither less pure nor less precious. Your heart would only be the more worthy of God, if, by its humility and annihilation, it attracted the succor that He was disposed to send. Is this the way you put off self? Is this the view that pure faith takes of the instrument of God? Is it thus that you die to the life of self within? To what purpose are your readings about pure love, and your frequent devotions? How can you read what condemns the very depths of your soul? You are influenced not only by self-interest, put by the persuasions of pride, when you reject the gifts of God, because they do not come in a shape to suit your taste. How can you pray? What is the language of God in the depths of your soul? He asks nothing but death, and you desire nothing but life. How can you put up to Him a prayer for his grace, with a restriction that He shall only send it by a channel demanding no sacrifice on your part but ministering to the gratification of your carnal pride?

LETTER X.

The discovery and death of self.

Yea, I joyfully consent that you call me your father! I am so and will be always; there needs only on your part a full and confident persuasion of it, which will come when your heart is enlarged. Self-love now shuts it up. We are in a strait place, indeed, when we are enclosed in self, but when we emerge from that prison, and enter into the immensity of God and the liberty of his children, we are set at large.

I am rejoiced to find that God has reduced you to a state of weakness. Your self-love can neither be convinced nor vanquished by any other means, ever finding secret resources and impenetrable retreats in your courage and ingenuity. It was hidden from your eyes, while it fed upon the subtle poison of an apparent generosity, by which you constantly sacrificed yourself for others. God has forced it to cry aloud, to come forth into open day, and display its excessive jealousy. O how painful, but how useful, are these seasons of weakness! While any self-love remains, we are afraid of its being revealed, but so long as the least symptom of it lurks in the most secret recesses of the heart, God pursues it, and by some infinitely merciful blow, forces it into the light. The poison then becomes the remedy; self-love, pushed to extremity, discovers itself in all its deformity by a transport of despair, and disgraces all the refinements, and dissipates the flattering illusions of a whole life. God sets before your eyes your idol, self. You behold it, and cannot turn your eyes away; and as you have no longer power over yourself, you cannot keep the sight from others.

Thus to exhibit self-love without its mask is the most mortifying punishment that can be inflicted. We no longer behold it wise, discreet, polite, self-possessed, and courageous in sacrificing itself for others; it is no longer the self-love whose nourishment consisted in the belief that it had need of nothing, and the persuasion that its greatness and generosity deserved a different name. It is the selfishness of a silly child, screaming at the loss of an apple; but it is far more tormenting, for it also weeps from rage that it has wept; it cannot be still, and refuses all comfort, because its venomous character has been detected. It beholds itself foolish, rude, and impertinent, and is forced to look its own frightful countenance in the face. It says with Job: "*For the thing which I greatly feared is come upon me, and that which I was afraid of is come unto me.*" (*Job*, iii. 25.) For precisely that which it most fears is the most necessary means of its destruction.

We have no need that God should attack in us what has neither life nor sensibility. It is the living only that must die, and all the rest is nought. This, then, is what you needed, to behold a self-love convinced, sensitive, gross, and palpable. And now all you have to do, is to be quietly willing to look at it as it is; the moment you can do this it will have disappeared.

You ask for a remedy, that you may get well. You do not need to be cured, but to be slain; seek not impatiently for a remedy, but let death come. Be careful, however, lest a certain courageous resolve to avail yourself of no remedy, be itself a remedy in disguise, and give aid and comfort to this cursed life. Seek no consolation for self-love, and do not conceal the disease. Reveal everything in simplicity and holiness, and then suffer yourself to die.

But this is not to be accomplished by any exertion of strength. Weakness is become your only possession; all strength is out of place; it only serves to render the agony longer and more distressing. If you expire from exhaustion, you will die so much the quicker and less violently. A dying life must of necessity be painful. Cordials are a cruelty to the sufferer on the wheel; he only longs for the fatal blow, not food, nor sustenance. If it were possible to weaken him and hasten his death, we should abridge his sufferings; but we can do nothing; the hand alone that tied him to his torture can deliver him from the remains of suffering life.

Ask, then, neither remedies, sustenance, nor death; to ask death, is impatience; to ask food or remedies is to prolong our agony. What, then, shall we do? Let alone; seek nothing, hold to nothing; confess everything, not as a means of consolation, but through humility and desire to yield. Look to me, not as a source of life, but as a means of death. As an instrument of life would belie its purpose, if it did not minister to life, so an instrument of death would be falsely named, if, in lieu of slaying, it kept alive. Let me, then, be, or at least seem to you to be, hard, unfeeling, indifferent, pitiless, wearied, annoyed, and contemptuous. God knows how far it is from the truth; but he permits it all to appear; and I shall be much more serviceable to you in this false and imaginary character than by my affection and real assistance, for the point is not, how you are to be sustained and kept alive, but how you are to lose all and die.

LETTER XL.

The sight of our imperfections should not take away our peace.

There is something very hidden and very deceptive in your suffering; for while you seem to yourself to be wholly occupied with the glory of God, in your inmost soul it is self alone that occasions all your trouble. You are, indeed, desirous that God should be glorified, but that it should take place by means of your perfection, and you thus cherish the sentiments of self-love. It is simply a refined pretext for dwelling in self. If you would truly derive profit from the discovery of your imperfections, neither justify nor condemn yourself on their account, but quietly lay them before God, conforming your will to his in all things that you cannot understand, and remaining at peace; for peace is the order of God for every condition whatever. There is, in fact, a peace of conscience which sinners themselves should enjoy when awakened to repentance. Their suffering should be peaceful and mingled with consolation. Remember the beautiful word which once delighted you, that the Lord was not in noise and confusion, but in the still, small voice. (1 *Kings*, xix. 11.)

LETTER XII.

Living by the cross and by faith.

Everything is a cross; I have no joy but bitterness; but the heaviest cross must be borne in peace. At times it can neither be borne nor dragged; we can only fall down beneath it, overwhelmed and exhausted. I pray that God may spare you as much as possible in apportioning your suffering; it is our daily bread; God alone knows how much we need; and we must live in faith upon the means of death, confident, though we see it not, that God, with secret compassion, proportions our trials to the unperceived succor that He administers within. This life of faith is the most penetrating of all deaths

LETTER XIII.

Despair at our imperfection is a greater obstacle than the imperfection itself

Be not concerned about your defects. Love without ceasing, and you shall be much forgiven, because you have loved much. (*Luke*, vii. 47.) We are apt to seek the delights and selfish supports of love, rather than love itself. We deceive ourselves, even in supposing we are endeavoring to love, when we are only trying to see that we love. We are more occupied with the love, says St. Francis of Sales, than with the Well-beloved. If He were our only object, we should be all taken up with Him; but when we are employed in obtaining an assurance of his love, we are still in a measure busy with self. Our defects, regarded in peace and in the spirit of love, are instantly consumed by love itself; but considered in the light of self, they make us restless, and interrupt the presence of God and the exercise of perfect love. The chagrin we feel at our own defects, is ordinarily a greater fault than the original defect itself. You are wholly taken up with the less of the two faults, like a person whom I have just seen, who, after reading the life of one of the saints, was so enraged at his own comparative imperfection, that he entirely abandoned the idea of living a devoted life. I judge of your fidelity by your peace and liberty of soul; the more peaceful and enlarged your heart, the nearer you seem to be to God.

LETTER XIV.

Pure faith sees God alone

Be not anxious about the future; it is opposed to grace. When God sends you consolation, regard Him only in it, enjoy it day by day as the Israelites received their manna, and do not endeavor to lay it up in store. There are two peculiarities of pure faith; it sees God alone under all the imperfect envelopes which conceal Him,* and it holds the soul incessantly in suspense. We are kept constantly in the air, without being suffered to touch a foot to solid ground. The comfort of the present instant will be wholly inappropriate to the next; we must let God act with the most perfect freedom, in whatever belongs to Him, and think only of being faithful in all that depends upon ourselves. This momentary dependence, this darkness and this peace of the soul, under the utter uncertainty of the future, is a true martyrdom, which takes place silently and without any stir. It is death by a slow fire; and

---

* The man that looks on glass,
   On it may stay his eye;
  Or, if he pleaseth, through it pass,
   And then the heavens espy.—Herbert.

Pure faith cannot see the neighbor that succeeds, as he blindly thinks, in injuring us, nor the disease that attacks our bodies; that would be to stay its eye upon the glass, in which it would see a thousand flaws and imperfections that would annoy it and destroy its peace; it looks right through and discovers God; and what He permits, it cannot but joyfully acquiesce in.—*Editor.*

the end comes so imperceptibly and interiorly, that it is often almost as much hidden from the sufferer himself, as from those who are unacquainted with his state. When God removes his gifts from you, He knows how and when to replace them, either by others or by Himself. He can raise up children from the very stones.

Eat then your daily bread without thought for the morrow; "*sufficient unto the day is the evil thereof.*" (*Matt.* vi. 34.) To-morrow will take thought for the things of itself. He who feeds you to-day, is the same to whom you will look for food to-morrow; manna shall fall again from Heaven in the midst of the desert, before the children of God shall want any good thing.

LETTER XV.

Our knowledge stands in the way of our becoming wise

LIVE in peace, my dear young lady, without any thought for the future; perhaps there will be none for you. You have no present, even, of your own, for you must only use it in accordance with the designs of God, to whom it truly belongs. Continue the good works that occupy you, since you have an attraction that way, and can readily accomplish them. Avoid distractions, and the consequences of your excessive vivacity, and, above all things, be faithful to the present moment, and you will receive all necessary grace.

It is not enough to be detached from the world;

we must become lowly also; in detachment, we renounce the things without, in lowliness, we abandon self. Every shadow of perceptible pride must be left behind, and the pride of wisdom and virtue is more dangerous than that of worldly fortune, as it has a show of right, and is more refined.

We must be lowly-minded in all points, and appropriate nothing to ourselves, our virtue and courage least of all. You rest too much in your own courage, disinterestedness, and uprightness. The babe owns nothing; it treats a diamond and an apple alike. Be a babe; have nothing of your own; forget yourself; give way on all occasions; let the smallest be greater than you.

Pray simply from the heart, from pure love, and not from the head, from the intellect alone.

Your true instruction is to be found in spoliation, deep recollection, silence of the whole soul before God, in renouncing your own spirit, and, in the love of lowliness, obscurity, feebleness, and annihilation. This ignorance is the accomplished teacher of all truth; knowledge cannot attain to it, or can reach it but superficially.

LETTER XVI.

Those who endeavor to injure us are to be loved and welcomed as the hand of God.

I SYMPATHIZE, as I ought, in all your troubles, but I can do nothing else except pray God that He would console you. You have great need of the gift of his Spirit to sustain you in your difficulties, and to restrain your natural vivacity under the trials which are so fitted to excite it. As to the letter touching your birth, I think you should lay it before God alone, and beg his mercy upo him who has sought to injure you.

I have always perceived, or thought that I perceived, that you were sensitive on that point. God always attacks us on our weak side; we do not aim to kill a person by striking a blow at his insensible parts, such as the hair or nails, but by endeavoring to reach at once the noble organs, the immediate seats of life. When God would have us die to self, he always touches the tenderest spot, that which is fullest of life. It is thus that he distributes crosses. Suffer yourself to be humbled. Silence and peace under humiliation are the true good of the soul; we are tempted, under a thousand specious pretexts, to speak humbly; but it is far better to be humbly silent. The humility that can yet talk, has need of careful watching; self-love derives comfort from its outward words.

Do not suffer yourself to get excited by what is said about you. Let the world talk; do you strive to do the will of God; as for that of men, you could never succeed in doing it to their satisfaction, and it is not worth the pains. A moment of silence, of peace, and of union to God, will amply recompense you for every calumny that shall be uttered against you. We must love our fellows, without expecting friendship from them; they leave us and return, they go and come; let them do as they will; it is but a feather, the sport of the wind. See God only in them; it is He that afflicts or consoles us, by means of them, according as we have need.

LETTER XVII.

Quietness in God our true resource

WARMTH of imagination, ardor of feeling, acuteness of reasoning, and fluency of expression, can do but little. The true agent is a perfect abandonment before God, in which we do everything by the light which He gives, and are content with the success which He bestows. This continual death is a blessed life known to few. A single word, uttered from this rest, will do more, even in outward affairs, than all our most eager and officious care. It is the Spirit of God that then speaks the word, and it loses none of its force and authority, but enlightens, persuades, moves, and edifies. We have accomplished everything, and have scarce said anything.

On the other hand, if left to the excitability of our natural temperament, we talk forever, indulging in a thousand subtle and superfluous reflections; we are constantly afraid of not saying or doing enough; we get angry, excited, exhausted, distracted, and finally make no headway. Your disposition has an especial need of these maxims; they are as necessary for your body as your soul, and your physician, and your spiritual adviser should act together.

Let the water flow beneath the bridge; let men be men, that is to say, weak, vain, inconstant, unjust, false, and presumptuous; let the world be the world still; you cannot prevent it. Let every one follow his own inclination and habits; you cannot recast them, and the best course is, to let them be as they are and bear with them. Do not think it strange when you witness unreasonableness and injustice; rest in peace in the bosom of God; He sees it all more clearly than you do, and yet permits it. Be content to do quietly and gently what it becomes you to do, and let everything else be to you as though it were not.

LETTER XVIII.

True friendships are founded only in God.

WE must be content with what God gives, without having any choice of our own. It is right that his will should be done, not ours; and that his should become ours without the least reservation, in order that it may be done on earth as it is done in heaven. This is a hundred times more valuable an attainment than to be engaged in the view or consolation of self.

O how near are we to each other when we are all united in God! How well do we converse when we have but a single will and a single thought in Him who is all things in us! Would you find your true friends, then? Seek them only in Him who is the single source of true and eternal friendship. Would you speak with or hear from them? Sink in silence into the bosom of Him who is the word, the life, and the soul of all those who speak and live the truth. You will find in Him not only every want supplied, but everything perfect, which you find so imperfect in the creatures in whom you confide.

LETTER XIX.

The cross a source of our pleasure

I SYMPATHIZE with all your distresses; but we must carry the cross with Christ in this transitory life. We shall soon have no time to suffer; we shall reign with God our consolation, who will have wiped away our tears with his own hand, and from before whose presence pain and sighing shall forever flee away. While this fleeting moment of trial is permitted us, let us not lose the slightest portion of the worth of the cross. Let us suffer in humility and in peace; our self-love exaggerates our distresses, and magnifies them in our imagination. A cross borne in simplicity, without the interference of self-love to augment it, is only half a cross. Suffering in this simplicity of love, we are not only happy in spite of the cross, but because of it; for love is pleased in suffering for the Well-beloved, and the cross which forms us into his image is a consoling bond of love.

LETTER XX.

The absence of feeling and the revelation of self no sufficient causes of distress.

I PRAY God that this new year may be full of grace and blessing to you. I am not surprised that you do not enjoy recollection as you did on being delivered from a long and painful agitation. Everything is liable to be exhausted. A lively disposition, accustomed to active exertion, soon languishes in solitude and inaction. For a great number of years you have been necessarily much distracted by external activity, and it was this circumstance that made me fear the effect of the life of abandonment upon you. You were at first in the fervor of your beginnings, when no difficulties appear formidable. You said with Peter, it is good for us to be here; but it is often with us as it was with him, that we know not what we say. (*Mark*, ix. 56.) In our moments of enjoyment, we feel as if we could do everything; in the time of temptation and discouragement, we think we can do nothing, and believe that all is lost. But we are alike deceived in both.

You should not be disturbed at any distraction that you may experience; the cause of it lay concealed within even when you felt such zeal for recollection. Your temperament and habits all conduce to making you active and eager. It was only weariness and exhaustion that caused you to relish an opposite life. But, by fidelity to grace, you will gradually become permanently introduced into the experience of which you have had a momentary taste. God bestowed it that you might see whither He would lead you; He then takes it away, that we may be made sensible that it does not belong to us; that we are neither able to procure nor preserve it, and that it is a gift of grace that must be asked in all humility.

Be not amazed at finding yourself sensitive, impatient, haughty, self-willed; you must be made to perceive that such is your natural disposition. We must bear the yoke of the daily confusion of our sins, says St. Augustin. We must be made to feel our weakness, our wretchedness, our inability to correct ourselves. We must despair of our own heart, and have no hope but in God. We must bear with ourselves, without flattering, and without neglecting a single effort for our correction.

We must be instructed as to our true character, while waiting for God's time to take it away. Let us become lowly under his all-powerful hand; yielding and manageable as often as we perceive any resistance in our will. Be silent as much as you can. Be in no haste to judge; suspend your decisions, your likes and dislikes. Stop at once when you become aware that your activity is hurried, and do not be too eager even for good things.

LETTER XXI.

The imperfection of others to be borne in love

It is a long while since I renewed the assurance of my attachment to you in our Lord. It is, nevertheless, greater than ever. I desire with all my heart that you may always find in your household the peace and consolation which you enjoyed in the beginning. To be content with even the best of people, we must be contented with little and bear a great deal. Those who are most perfect, have many imperfections, and we have great faults, so that between the two, mutual toleration becomes very difficult. We must bear one another's burdens, and so fulfil the law of Christ, (*Gal.* vi. 2,) thus setting off one against the other in love. Peace and unanimity will be much aided by frequent silence, habitual recollection, prayer, self-abandonment, renunciation of all vain criticisms, and a faithful departure from the vain reflections of a jealous and difficult self-love. To how much trouble would this simplicity put an end! Happy he who neither listens to self nor to the tales of others!

Be content with leading a simple life, according to your condition. Be obedient, and bear your daily cross; you need it, and it is bestowed by the pure mercy of God. The grand point is to despise self from the heart, and to be willing to be despised, if God permits it. Feed upon Him alone; St. Augustin says that his mother lived upon prayer; do you do so likewise, and die to everything else. We can only live to God by the continual death of self.

LETTER XXII.

The fear of death not taken away by our own courage but by the grace of God

I AM not in the least surprised to learn that your impression of death becomes more lively, in proportion as age and infirmity bring it nearer. I experience the same thing. There is an age at which death is forced upon our consideration more frequently, by more irresistible reflections, and by a time of retirement in which we have fewer distractions. God makes use of this rough trial to undeceive us in respect to our courage, to make us feel our weakness, and to keep us in all humility in his own hands.

Nothing is more humiliating than a troubled imagination, in which we search in vain for our former confidence in God. This is the crucible of humiliation, in which the heart is purified by a sense of its weakness and unworthiness. In his sight shall no man living be justified (*Psalm* cxliii. 2); yea, the heavens are not clean in his sight, (*Job*, xv. 15,) and in many things we offend all. (*James*, iii. 2.) We behold our faults and not our virtues; which latter it would be even dangerous to behold, if they are real.

We must go straight on through this deprivation

without interruption, just as we were endeavoring to walk in the way of God, before being disturbed. If we should perceive any fault that needs correction, we must be faithful to the light given us, but do it carefully, lest we be led into false scruples. We must then remain at peace, not listening to the voice of self-love, mourning over our approaching death, but detach ourselves from life, offering it in sacrifice to God, and confidently abandon ourselves to Him. St. Ambrose was asked, when dying, whether he was not afraid of the judgments of God; "We have a good master," said he, and so must we reply to ourselves. We need to die in the most impenetrable uncertainty, not only as to God's judgment upon us, but as to our own characters. We must, as St. Augustin has it, be so reduced as to have nothing to present before God but *our wretchedness and his mercy*. Our wretchedness is the proper object of his mercy, and his mercy is all our merit. In your hours of sadness, read whatever will strengthen your confidence and establish your heart. "*Truly God is good to Israel, even to such as are of a clean heart.*" (*Psalm* lxxiii. 1.) Pray for this cleanness of heart, which is so pleasing in his sight, and which renders Him so compassionate to our failings.

LETTER XXIII.

Sensitiveness under reproof the surest sign we needed it.

I GREATLY desire that you may have interior peace. You know that it cannot be found, except in lowliness of mind, and lowliness is not real, except it be produced by God upon every proper occasion. These occasions are chiefly when we are blamed by some one who disapproves of us, and when we experience inward weakness. We must accustom ourselves to bearing both these trials.

We are truly lowly when we are no longer taken by surprise at finding ourselves corrected from without and incorrigible within. We are then like little children, below everything, and are willing to be so; we feel that our reprovers are right, but that we are unable to overcome ourselves, in order to correct our faults. Then we despair of ourselves, and expect nothing except from God; the reproofs of others, harsh and unfeeling as they may be, seem to us less than we deserve; if we cannot bear them, we condemn our sensitiveness more than all our other imperfections. Correction cannot then make us more humble than it finds us. The interior rebellion, far from hindering the profit of the correction, convinces us of its absolute necessity; in truth, the reproof would not have been felt, if it had not cut into some living part; had death been there, we should not have perceived it;

and thus the more acutely we feel, the more certainly we know that the correction was necessary.

I beg your forgiveness if I have said anything too harsh; but do not doubt my affection for you, and count as nothing everything that comes from me. See only the hand of God, which makes use of the awkwardness of mine, to deal you a painful blow. The pain proves that I have touched a sore spot. Yield to God, acquiesce in all his dealings, and you will soon be at rest and in harmony within. You know well enough how to give this advice to others; the occasion is important, critical. O what grace will descend upon you, if you will bear, like a little child, all the means God employs to humiliate and dispossess you of your senses and will! I pray that He may so diminish you that you can no longer be found at all.

LETTER XXIV.

Imperfection only is intolerant of imperfection

It has seemed to me that you have need of more enlargedness of heart in relation to the defects of others. I know that you cannot help seeing them when they come before you, nor prevent the opinions you involuntarily form concerning the motives of some of those about you. You cannot even get rid of a certain degree of trouble which these things cause you. It will be enough if you are willing to bear with those defects which are unmistakable, refrain from condemning those which are doubtful, and not suffer yourself to be so afflicted by them as to cause a coolness of feeling between you.

Perfection is easily tolerant of the imperfections of others; it becomes all things to all men. We must not be surprised at the greatest defects in good souls, and must quietly let them alone until God gives the signal of gradual removal; otherwise we shall pull up the wheat with the tares. God leaves, in the most advanced souls, certain weaknesses entirely disproportioned to their eminent state. As workmen, in excavating the soil from a field, leave certain pillars of earth which indicate the original level of the surface, and serve to measure the amount of material removed—God, in the same way, leaves pillars of testimony to the extent of his work in the most pious souls.

Such persons must labor, each one in his degree, for his own correction, and you must labor to bear with their weaknesses. You know from experience the bitterness of the work of correction; strive then to find means to make it less bitter to others. You have not an eager zeal to correct, but a sensitiveness that easily shuts up your heart.

I pray you more than ever not to spare my faults. If you should think you see one, which is not really there, there is no harm done; if I find that your counsel wounds me, my sensitiveness demonstrates that you have discovered a sore spot; but if not, you will have done me an excellent kindness in exercising my humility, and accustoming me to reproof. I ought to be more lowly than others in proportion as I am higher in position, and God demands of me a more absolute death to everything. I need this simplicity, and I trust it will be the means of cementing rather than of weakening our attachment.

LETTER XXV.

We should listen to God and not to self-love.

I BESEECH you not to listen to self. Self-love whispers in one ear and the love of God in the other; the first is restless, bold, eager, and impetuous; the other is simple, peaceful, and speaks but a few words in a mild and gentle voice. The moment we attend to the voice of self crying in our ear, we can no longer hear the modest tones of holy love. Each speaks only of its single object. Self-love entertains us with self, which, according to it, is never sufficiently well attended to; it talks of friendship, regard, esteem, and is in despair at everything but flattery. The love of God, on the other hand, desires that self should be forgotten, that it should be counted as nothing, that God might be all; that it should be trodden under foot and broken as an idol, and that God should become the self of espoused souls, and occupy them as others are occupied by self. Let the vain, complaining babbler, self-love, be silenced, that in the stillness of the heart we may listen to that other **love** that only speaks when addressed.

LETTER XXVI.

Absolute trust the shortest road to God

I HAVE no doubt but that God constantly treats you as one of his friends, that is, with crosses, sufferings, and humiliations. The ways and means of God to draw souls to Himself, accomplish his design much more rapidly and effectually than all the efforts of the creature; for they destroy self-love at its very root, where, with all our pains, we could scarce discover it. God knows all its windings, and attacks it in its strongest holds.

If we had strength and faith enough to trust ourselves entirely to God, and follow Him simply wherever He should lead us, we should have no need of any great effort of mind to reach perfection. But as we are so weak in faith, as to require to know all the way without trusting in God, our road is lengthened and our spiritual affairs get behind. Abandon yourself as absolutely as possible to God, and continue **to do so to** your latest breath, and He will never desert you.

LETTER XXVII.

The time of temptation and distress is no time to form resolves.

Your excessive distress is like a summer torrent, which must be suffered to run away. Nothing makes any impression upon you, and you think you have the most substantial evidence for the most imaginary states; it is the ordinary result of great suffering. God permits you, notwithstanding your excellent faculties, to be blind to what lies immediately before you, and to think you see clearly what does not exist at all. God will be glorified in your heart, if you will be faithful in yielding to his designs. But nothing would be more injudicious than the forming of resolutions in a state of distress, which is manifestly accompanied by an inability to do anything according to God.

When you shall have become calm, then do in a spirit of recollection, what you shall perceive to be nearest the will of God respecting you. Return gradually to devotion, simplicity, and the oblivion of self. Commune and listen to God, and be deaf to self. Then do all that is in your heart, for I have no fear that a spirit of that sort will permit you to take any wrong step. But to suppose that we are sane when we are in the very agony of distress, and under the influence of a violent temptation of self-love, is to ensure our being led astray. Ask any experienced adviser, and he will tell you that you are to make no resolutions until you have re-entered into peace and recollection. You will learn from him that the readiest way to self-deception is, to trust to ourselves in a state of suffering, in which nature is so unreasonable and irritated.

You will say that I desire to prevent you doing as you ought, if I forbid your doing it at the only moment when you are capable of it. God forbid! I neither desire to permit nor hinder: my only wish is so to advise you that you shall not be found wanting toward God. Now it is as clear as day, that you would fail in that respect, if you took counsel at the hands of a self-love wounded to the quick, and an irritation verging upon despair. Would you change anything to gratify your self-love, when God does not desire it? God forbid! Wait, then, until you shall be in a condition to be advised. To enjoy the true advantages of illumination, we must be equally ready for every alternative, and must have nothing which we are not cheerfully disposed at once to sacrifice for His sake.

LETTER XXVIII.

Who has love, has all.

I HAVE thought frequently, since yesterday, on the matters you communicated to me, and I have increasing confidence that God will sustain you. Though you take no great pleasure in religious exercises, you must dot neglect to be faithful in them, as far as your health will permit. A convalescent has but little appetite, but he must eat to sustain life.

It would be very serviceable to you, if you could occasionally have a few minutes of Christian converse with such of your family as you can confide in, and, as to the choice, be guided in perfect liberty by your impressions at the moment. God does not call you by any lively emotions, and I heartily rejoice at it, if you will but remain faithful; for a fidelity, unsustained by delights, is far purer, and safer from danger, than one accompanied by those tender feelings, which may be seated too exclusively in the imagination. A little reading and recollection every day, will be the means of insensibly giving you light and strength for all the sacrifices God will require of you. Love Him, and I will acquit you of everything else; for everything else will come by love. I do not ask from you a love tender and emotional, but only that your will should lean towards love, and that, notwithstanding all the corrupt desires of your heart, you should prefer God before self and the whole world.

LETTER XXIX.

Weakness preferable to strength, and practice better than knowledge

I AM told, my dear child in our Lord, that you are suffering from sickness. I suffer with you, for I love you dearly; but I cannot but kiss the hand that smites you, and I pray you to kiss it lovingly with me. You have heretofore abused your health and the pleasures derived from it; this weakness and its attendant pains are the natural consequence of such a course.

I pray God only that He may depress your spirit even more than your body, and while He comforts the latter according to your need, that He may entirely vanquish the former. O how strong we are when we begin to perceive that we are but weakness and infirmity! Then we are ever ready to believe that we are mistaken, and to correct ourselves while confessing it; our minds are ever open to the illumination of others; then we are authoritative in nothing, and say the most decided things with simplicity and deference for others; then we do not object to be judged, and submit without hesitation to the censure of the first comer. At the same time, we judge no one without absolute necessity; we speak only to those who desire it, mentioning the imperfections we seem to have discovered, without dogmatism, and rather to gratify their wishes than from a desire to be believed or create a reputation for wisdom.

I pray God that He may keep you faithful to his grace, and that He who hath begun a good work in you will perform it until the day of Jesus Christ. (*Phil.* i. 6.) We must bear with ourselves with patience and without flattery, and remain in unceasing subjection to every means of overcoming our thoughts and inward repugnances; we shall tl us become more pliable to the impressions of grace in the practice of the gospel. But let this work be done quietly and peacefully, and let it not be entered upon too eagerly, as though it could all be accomplished in a single day Let us *reason* little, but *do* much. If we are not careful, the acquisition of knowledge will so occupy this life that we shall need another to reduce our acquirements into practice. We are in danger of believing ourselves advanced towards perfection in proportion to our knowledge* of the way; but all our beautiful theories, far from assisting in the death of self, only serve to nourish the life of Adam in us by a secret delight and confidence in our illumination. Be quit then of all trust in your own power and in your own knowl-

---

* This seems one of the most common as well as most serious mistakes to which spiritual persons are liable. God gives the knowledge and desires us to put it in practice; but the moment we see it, we are so carried away with delight, that we forget that there is anything else to be done; whereas we have comparatively slender reason to rejoice until it is put in vital operation in the life. Ye *see*, says the Saviour, but do not *perceive*, ye *hear*, but do not *understand*. Food, lying undigested in the stomach, is not only of no service to the body, but if not removed, will become a serious injury; it is only when it is assimilated and mingled with the blood, and when it appears by its good effects in our hands, feet, head, and trunk, that it can be said to have become our own. To have a divine truth in the intellect, is indeed matter of thanksgiving; but it will avail only to our condemnation, if it be not also loved in the heart and acted in the life. Let us remember that it is not the *knowledge* of the way that God desires in us, but the *practice* of it; not *light*, but *love*. For though I understand all mysteries and *all knowlegde*—and have not charity—I am nothing. (1 *Cor.* xiii, 2.)—*Editor.*

edge of the way, and you will make a great stride towards perfection. Humility and self-distrust, with a frank ingenuousness, are fundamental virtues for you.

LETTER XXX.

Beware of the pride of reasoning; the true guide to knowledge is love

Your mind is too much occupied with exterior things, and still worse, with argumentation, to be able to act with a frequent thought of God. I am always afraid of your excessive inclination to reason; it is a hinderance to that recollection and silence in which He reveals Himself. Be humble, simple, and sincerely abstracted with men; be recollected, calm, and devoid of reasonings before God. The persons who have heretofore had most influence with you, have been infinitely dry, reasoning, critical, and opposed to a true interior life. However little you might listen to them, you would hear only endless reasonings and a dangerous curiosity, which would insensibly draw you out of Grace and plunge you into the depths of Nature. Habits of long standing are easily revived; and the changes which cause us to revert to our original position are less easily perceived, because they are natural to our constitution. Distrust them, then; and beware of beginnings which, in fact, include the end.

It is now four months since I have had any leisure for study; but I am very happy to forego study, and not to cling to anything, when Providence would take it away. It may be that during the coming winter I shall have leisure for my library, but I shall enter it then, keeping one foot on the threshold, ready to leave it at the slightest intimation. The mind must keep fasts as well as the body. I have no desire to write, or speak, or to be spoken about, or to reason, or to persuade any. I live every day aridly enough, and with certain exterior inconveniences which beset me; but I amuse myself whenever I have an opportunity, if I need recreation. Those who make almanacs upon me, and are afraid of me, are sadly deceived. God bless them! I am far from being so foolish as to incommode myself for the sake of annoying them. I would say to them as Abraham said to Lot: *Is not the whole land before thee?* If you go to the east, I will go to the west. (*Gen.* xiii. 9.)

Happy he who is indeed free! The Son of God alone can make us free; but He can only do it by snapping every bond; and how is this to be done? By that sword which divides husband and wife, father and son, brother and sister. The world is then no longer of any account; but, as long as it is anything to us, so long our freedom is but a word, and we are as easily captured as a bird whose leg is fastened by a thread. He seems to be free; the string is not visible; but he can only fly its length, and he is a prisoner. You see the moral. What I would have you possess is more valuable than all you are fearful of losing. Be faithful in what you know, that you may be entrusted with more. Distrust your intellect, which has so often misled you. My own has been such a deceiver, that I no longer count upon it. Be simple, and firm in your simplicity. "*The fashion of this world passeth away.*" (1 *Cor.* vii. 31.) We shall vanish with it, if we make ourselves like it by reason of vanity; but the truth of God remains forever, and we shall dwell with it if it alone occupies our attention.

Again I warn you, beware of philosophers and great reasoners. They will always be a snare to you, and will do you more harm than you will know how to do them good. They linger and pine away in discussing exterior trifles, and never reach the knowledge of the truth. Their curiosity is an insatiable spiritual avarice. They are like those conquerors who ravage the world without possessing it. Solomon, after a deep experience of it, testifies to the vanity of their researches.

We should never study but on an express intimation of Providence; and we should do it as we go to market, to buy the provision necessary for each day's wants. Then, too, we must study in the spirit of prayer. God is, at the same time, the Truth and the Love. We can only know the truth in proportion as we love—when we love it, we understand it well. If we do not love Love, we do not know Love. He who loves much, and remains humble and lowly in his ignorance, is the well-beloved one of the Truth;

he knows what philosophers not only are ignorant of, but do not desire to know. Would that you might obtain that knowledge which is reserved for *babes and the simple-minded*, while it is hid from the *wise and prudent*. (Matt. xi. 25.)

LETTER XXXI.

The gifts of God not to be rejected on account of the channel that brings them

I AM glad you find in the person of whom you speak, the qualities you were in search of. God puts what He pleases where He pleases. Naaman could not be healed by all the waters of Syria, but must apply to those of Palestine. What does it matter from what quarter our light and help come? The source is the important point, not the conduit; that is the best channel which most exercises our faith, puts to shame our human wisdom, makes us simple and humble, and undeceives us in respect to our own power. Receive, then, whatever He bestows, in dependerce upon the Spirit that bloweth where it listeth. We know not whence it cometh nor whither it goeth. (*John*, iii. 8.) But we need not seek to know the secrets of God; let us only be obedient to what He reveals.

Too much reasoning is a great distraction. Those who reason—the indevout wise—quench the inward spirit as the wind extinguishes a candle. After being with them for awhile, we perceive our hearts dry, and our mind off its centre. Shun intercourse with such men; they are full of danger to you.

There are some who appear recollected, but whose appearance deceives us. It is easy to mistake a certain warmth of the imagination for recollection. Such persons are eager in the pursuit of some outward good, to which they are attached; they are distracted by this anxious desire; they are perpetually occupied in discussions and reasonings, but know nothing of that inward peace and silence, that listens to God. They are more dangerous than others, because their distraction is more disguised. Search their depths, and you will find them restless, fault-finding, eager, constantly occupied without, harsh and crude in all their desires, sensitive, full of their own thoughts, and impatient of the slightest contradiction; in a word, spiritual busybodies, annoyed at everything, and almost always annoying.

LETTER XXXII.

Poverty and spoliation the way of Christ.

EVERYTHING contributes to prove you; but God who loves you, will not suffer your temptations to exceed your strength. He will make use of the trial for your advancement. But we must not look inwards with curiosity to behold our progress, our strength, or the hand of God, which is not the less efficient because it is invisible. Its principal operations are conducted in secrecy, for we should never die to self, if He always visibly stretched out his hand to save us. God would then sanctify us in light, life and the possession of every spiritual grace; but not upon the cross, in darkness, privation, nakedness and death. The directions of Christ are not, if any one will come after me, let him enjoy himself, let him be gorgeously apparelled, let him be intoxicated with delight, as was Peter on the mount, let him be glad in his perfection in me and in himself, let him behold himself, and be assured that he is perfect; on the contrary, his words are; *If any one will come after me,* I will show him the road he must take; *let him deny himself, take up his cross and follow me* in a path beside precipices, where he will see nothing but death on every hand. (*Matt.* xvi. 24.) St. Paul declares that we desire to be clothed upon, and that it is necessary, on the contrary, to be stripped to very nakedness, that we may then put on Christ.

Suffer Him, then, to despoil self-love of every adornment, even to the inmost covering under which it lurks, that you may receive the robe whitened by the blood of the Lamb, and having no other purity than his. O happy soul, that no longer possesses anything of its own, nor even anything borrowed, and that abandons itself to the Well-beloved, being jealous of every beauty but his? O spouse, how beautiful art thou, when thou hast no longer anything of thine own! Thou shalt be altogether the delight of the bridegroom, when He shall be all thy comeliness!

Then He will love thee without measure, because it will be Himself that He loves in thee.

Hear these things and believe them. This pure truth shall be bitter in your mouth and belly, but it shall feed your heart upon that death which is the only true life. Give faith to this, and listen not to self; it is the grand seducer, more powerful than the serpent that deceived our mother. Happy the soul that hearkens in all simplicity to the voice that forbids its hearing or compassionating self!

LETTER XXXIII.

The will of God our only treasure.

I DESIRE that you may have that absolute simplicity of abandonment that never measures its own extent, nor excepts anything in the present life, no matter how dear to our self-love. All illusions come, not from such an abandonment as this, but from one attended by secret reservations.

Be as lowly and simple in the midst of the most exacting society as in your own closet. Do nothing from the reasonings of wisdom, nor from natural pleasure, but all from submission to the Spirit of life and death; death to self, and life in God. Let there be no enthusiasm, no search after certainty within, no looking forwards for better things, as if the present, bitter as it is, were not sufficient to those whose sole treasure is the will of God, and as if you would indemnify self-love for the sadness of the present by the prospects of the future! We deserve to meet with disappointment when we seek such vain consolation. Let us receive everything in lowliness of spirit, seeking nothing from curiosity, and withholding nothing from a disguised selfishness. Let God work, and think only of dying to the present moment without reservation, as though it were the whole of eternity.

LETTER XXXIV.

Abandonment not a heroic sacrifice, but a simple sinking into the will of God.

Your sole task, my dear daughter, is, to bear your infirmities both of body and mind. *When I am weak*, says the Apostle, *then am I strong;* strength is made perfect in weakness. We are only strong in God in proportion as we are weak in ourselves; your feebleness will be your strength if you accept it in all lowliness.

We are tempted to believe that weakness and lowliness are incompatible with abandonment, because this latter is represented as a generous act of the soul by which it testifies its great love, and makes the most heroic sacrifices. But a true abandonment does not at all correspond to this flattering description; it is a simple resting in the love of God, as an infant lies in its mother's arms. A perfect abandonment must even go so far as to abandon its abandonment. We renounce ourselves without knowing it; if we knew it, it would no longer be complete, for there can be no greater support than a consciousness that we are wholly given up.

Abandonment consists, not in doing great things for self to take delight in, but simply in suffering our weakness and infirmity, in letting everything alone. It is peaceful, for it would no longer be sincere, if we were still restless about anything we had renounced. It is thus that abandonment is the source of true peace; if we have not peace, it is because our abandonment is exceedingly imperfect.

LETTER XXXV.

Daily dying takes the place of final death.

WE must bear our crosses; self is the greatest of them; we are not entirely rid of it until we can tolerate ourselves as simply and patiently as we do our neighbor. If we die in part every day of our lives, we shall have but little to do on the last. What we so much dread in the future will cause us no fear when it comes, if we do not suffer its terrors to be exaggerated by the restless anxieties of self-love. Bear with yourself, and consent in all lowliness to be supported by your neighbor. O how utterly will these little daily deaths destroy the power of the final dying!

LETTER XXXVI.

Suffering belongs to the living, not the dead

MANY are deceived when they suppose that the death of self is the cause of all the agony they feel, but their suffering is only caused by the remains of life. Pain is seated in the living, not the dead parts; the more suddenly and completely we expire, the less pain do we experience. Death is only painful to him who resists it; the imagination exaggerates its terrors; the spirit argues endlessly to show the propriety of the life of self; self-love fights against death, like a sick man in the last struggle. But we must die inwardly as well as outwardly; the sentence of death has gone forth against the spirit as well as against the body. Our great care should be that the spirit die first, and then our bodily death will be but a falling asleep. Happy they who sleep this sleep of peace!

LETTER XXXVII.

The limits of our grace are those of our temptation

I SYMPATHISE sincerely with the sufferings of your dear sick one, and with the pain of those whom God has placed about her to help her bear the cross. Let her not distrust God, and He will proportion her suffering to the patience which He will bestow. No one can do this but He who made all hearts, and whose office it is to renew them by his grace. The man in whom He operates, knows nothing of the proper proportions; and, seeing the extent, neither of his future trials, nor of the grace prepared to meet them, he is tempted to discouragement and despair. Like a man who had never seen the ocean, he stands, at the coming in of the tide, between the water and an impassable wall of rock, and thinks he perceives the terrible certainty that the approaching waves must surely engulf him; he does not see that he stands within the point, at which God, with unerring finger, has drawn their boundary-line, and beyond which they shall not pass.

God proves the righteous as with the ocean; he stirs it up, and makes its great billows seem to threaten our destruction, but He is always at hand to say, thus far shalt thou go and no farther. "*God is faithful, who will not suffer you to be tempted above that ye are able.*" (1 *Cor.* x. 13.)

LETTER XXXVIII.

Resisting God, an effectual bar to grace

You perceive, by the light of God, in the depth of your conscience, what grace demands of you, but you resist Him. Hence your distress. You begin to say within, it is impossible for me to undertake to do what is required of me; this is a temptation to despair. Despair as much as you please of self, but never of God; He is all good and all powerful, and will grant you according to your faith. If you will believe all things, all things shall be yours, and you shall remove mountains. If you believe nothing, you shall have nothing, but you alone will be to blame. Look at Abraham, who hoped against every rational hope! Look at Mary, who, when the most incredible thing in the world was proposed to her, did not hesitate, but exclaimed; "*be it unto me according to thy word.*" (*Luke*, i. 38.)

Open, then, your heart. It is now so shut up, that you not only have not the power to do what is required of you, but you do not even desire to have it; you have no wish that your heart should be enlarged, and you fear that it will be. How can grace find room in so straitened a heart? All that I ask of you is, that you will rest in a teachable spirit of faith, and that you will not listen to self. Simply acquiesce in everything with lowliness of mind, and receive peace through recollection, and everything will be gradually accomplished for you; those things which, in your hour of temptation, seemed the greatest difficulties, will be insensibly smoothed away.

LETTER XXXIX.

God speaks more effectually IN the soul, than TO it.

Nothing gives me more satisfaction than to see you simple and peaceful. Simplicity brings back the state of Paradise. We have no great pleasures, and suffer some pain; but we have no desire for the former, and we receive the latter with thanksgiving. This interior harmony, and this exemption from the fears and tormenting desires of self-love, create a satisfaction in the will, which is above all the joys of intoxicating delights. Dwell, then, in your terrestrial paradise, and take good care not to leave it from a vain desire of knowing good and evil.

We are never less alone than when we are in the society of a single faithful friend; never less deserted. than when we are carried in the arms of the Allpowerful. Nothing is more affecting than the instant succor of God. What He sends by means of his creatures, contracts no virtue from that foul and barren channel; it owes everything to the source. And so, when the fountain breaks forth within the heart itself, we have no need of the creature. "*God, who at sundry times and in divers manners, spake in time past unto the fathers by the prophets, hath, in these last days, spoken unto us by his Son.*" (*Heb.* i. 1, 2.) Shall we then feel any regret that the feeble voice of the prophets has ceased? O how pure and powerful is the immediate voice of God in the soul! It is certain whenever Providence cuts off all the channels.

LETTER XL.

The circumcision of the heart

Our eagerness to serve others, frequently arises from mere natural generosity and a refined self-love; it may soon turn into dislike and despair. But true charity is simple, and ever the same towards the neighbor, because it is humble, and never thinks of self. Whatever is not included in this *pure charity*, must be cut off.

It is by the circumcision of the heart that we are made children and inheritors of the faith of Abraham, in order that we may, like him, quit our native country without knowing whither we go. Blessed lot! to leave all and deliver ourselves up to the jealousy of God, the knife of circumcision! Our own hand can effect nothing but superficial reforms; we do not know ourselves, and cannot tell where to strike; we should never light upon the spot that the hand of God so readily finds. Self-love arrests our hand and spares itself; it has not the courage to wound itself to the quick. And besides, the choice of the spot and the preparation for the blow, deaden its force. But the hand of God strikes in unexpected places, it finds the very joint of the harness, and leaves nothing unscathed. Self-love then becomes the patient; let it cry out, but see to it that it does not stir under the hand of God, lest it interfere with the success of the operation. It must remain motionless beneath the knife; all that is required is fidelity in not refusing a single stroke.

I am greatly attached to John Baptist, who wholly forgot himself that he might think only of Christ; he pointed to Him, he was but the voice of one crying in the wilderness to prepare the way, he sent Him all his disciples, and it was this conduct, far more than his solitary and austere life, that entitled him to be called the greatest among them **that are born of women.**

www.ingramcontent.com/pod-product-compliance
Lightning Source LLC
Chambersburg PA
CBHW011951150426
43195CB00018B/2892